This book is dedicated to all who find Nature not an adversary to conquer and destroy, but a storehouse of infinite knowledge and experience linking man to all things past and present. They know conserving the natural environment is essential to our future well-being.

VIRGIN ISLANDS
NATIONAL PARK
THE STORY BEHIND THE SCENERY®

by Alan H. Robinson Former Marine Research Biologist, Virgin Islands National Park
with Fritz Henle Photographer

A career employee of the National Park Service, Alan Robinson is active in the development and preservation of coastal and marine parks. He holds a degree in biological oceanography from Scripps Institution of Oceanography. Mr. Robinson's research and planning efforts include aquatic studies in North America, Africa, and the Caribbean.

Fritz Henle — whose reputation as a photographer is international — has lived in the Virgin Islands for many years. Mr. Henle's photography was instrumental in laying the groundwork for the national park on St. John, and he continues through his creative efforts to work energetically for the Caribbean and its people.

Underwater Photography by Clarendon Bowman

Edited by Gwen DenDooven, Book Design by K. C. DenDooven

VIRGIN ISLANDS NATIONAL PARK — THE STORY BEHIND THE SCENERY. PUBLISHED BY KC PUBLICATIONS, P.O. BOX 14883, LAS VEGAS, NEVADA 89114. SOFTCOVER EDITION, $2.50. L.C. NUMBER 74-81560.
Printed in the United States of America

Glistening bays, tucked away like jewels along the coral-bounded coast — vine-entangled ruins of man's experiments with nature — a rugged land and the all-embracing sea, rampant with life: here is a world where one can feel an overwhelming sense of the timelessness of nature and man's place within it.

Jutting eastward from Central America's Yucatan Peninsula, a great submarine mountain range rises from the ocean floor. Forming the northern boundary of the Caribbean Sea, these mountains break the surface in a succession of major subtropical islands known as the Greater Antilles. At the eastward end of that chain, like fragments floating gracefully in the wake of neighboring Puerto Rico, lies the assemblage Columbus romantically likened in number and purity to St. Ursala's 11,000 virgins.

Actually numbering far fewer than this, the group has only four islands of any size — the mountainous St. Thomas, St. John, Tortola, and Virgin Gorda. They are surrounded by several score of lesser cays, bearing names reminiscent of the colorful cultural history of the area—Fallen Jerusalem, Dead Chest, Dutch Cap, Le Duck, and Durloe. The story told here concerns St. John, the island said by some to be the most favored of the Virgins.

Although its authorized boundaries include two-thirds of the entire island of St. John, Virgin Islands National Park is actually the smallest of the "natural area" national parks of the United States. Yet, within its 9,500 areas of rugged landscape and 5,650 acres of surrounding waters, this small park brings together a remarkable and enlightening array of cultural and natural histories.

The Sea and Shore — The clear, warm waters surrounding St. John support a diverse and intriguing complex of coral reefs whose well-being is closely tied to its own plant and animal components, to nearby sand and grass-bed communities, and to the energies of passing waves and currents. The island's fine beaches of coral sand depend directly on continued reef health for their existence. Man, in his use or misuse of the land and water above, is a major factor in the survival of the reefs.

The Island — Born quietly on a deep ocean floor, St. John was later brought to the surface, where an exposive period of volcanic eruption and centuries of coral-reef deposits laid down the complex series of rocks exposed today. Faulting, weathering, and a mantle of subtropical vegetation have softened its once jagged profile.

The People — In the past, as today, the people of St. John have lived in close union with the sea and land. In artifact, lore, and attitude they have left this generation much to ponder and much to respect.

From the coast above, as many visitors first perceive them, the coral reefs of St. John appear only as indistinct, dark patches, giving little hint of the beautiful complexity fundamental to living communities. Rich and exciting biological habitats in themselves, these reefs exert a profound physica influence throughout the adjacent shallow-water and coastal environment of St. John. The island's sandy beaches and quiet lagoons — even its man-

Hawksnest Bay

The Sea and Shore

grove swamps and coastal saltponds — owe their existence in part to past and present living coral reefs.

CORAL — THE LIVING ROCK

The term *coral reef* does not refer to any single species of plant or animal, but rather to an integrated community, a functioning assemblage of a large variety of organisms. Some of the units within the reef system — the so-called stony or hard corals and certain algae — are directly responsible for depositing within their tissues the insoluble carbonate material of the reef. Other forms — like the soft-bodied sponges, sea urchins, burrowing worms, and certain fish species — act to break down, rearrange, and aid in cementing this material into a solid basement layer on which coral growth continues.

This continual breakdown and sorting also results in an important by-product: sand-sized particles and larger fragments which are moved by waves and currents to the surrounding bottom communities and to the shore. If they did not provide themselves with additional substrate for growth, adjacent corals would soon crowd each other to a standstill; and, without the export of excess sand and debris, the reef would eventually be smothered in its own carbonate wastes.

The fundamental construction unit of the reef is the coral animal itself, a colonial relative of common sea anemones. A tiny hollow cylinder of tissue crowned by contractile tentacles, the coral polyp secretes a hard skeletal cup of calcium carbonate outside its soft body.

The polyp feeds mainly at night. It is capable of taking in live food (primarily living planktonic organisms) drifting within reach of its tentacles, which are equipped with special stinging and holding cells to trap such prey. Ciliated cells in the "throat" of the polyp help set up water currents which bring in even finer particles, all eventually passing into the central digestive cavity.

A second energy pathway — one of major importance in the depth and geographic distribution of reefs — involves algae (*zooxanthellae*) growing within the polyp tissues. Individually microscopic,

Stout vertical columns rising from an expanded base are characteristic of PILLAR CORAL (Dendrogyra cylindrus), a hard coral found in shallow, turbulent water where more fragile forms could not survive.

The individual polyps of living coral animals generally remain tightly closed during daylight hours, opening only at night to feed. The common STAR CORAL (Montastrea cavernosa), which forms massive heads at depths below the surf zone, opens at night (above) with an impressive array of tentacle-ringed "mouths" to capture floating plankton organisms. Energy stored up by the coral's internal plant-like cells during daylight makes this nightly feeding possible.

many thousands of these algal cells may be found in a single polyp, where they are collectively responsible for the coral colony's rich color scheme.

During hours of sunlight, and where water clarity permits adequate light penetration, these zooxanthellae take up carbon dioxide and photosynthesize like other plants, producing oxygen and manufacturing organic compounds of benefit to themselves and to the host coral animal. This relationship is symbiotic, not parasitic, since the the benefits are mutual: The polyp provides a safe, stable niche for the algae and in return receives an internal supply of oxygen and organic nutrients.

Corals denied the benefits of this symbiosis, such as those in deep, dark waters or those in which the algae may have been killed by a temporary loss of sunlight, grow very slowly or do not survive at all. Probably reflecting their evolutionary history as free-living planktonic organisms, most zooxanthellae may still temporarily become free-swimming, flagellated cells outside a host polyp.

The process of growth of an individual colony

The tentacles of PILLAR CORAL may be expanded day and night, giving a soft, furry appearance.

In BRAIN CORALS (e.g.: Diploria labyrinthiformis) the polyps are located along sinuous meandering rows separated by hard ridges.

NPS PHOTO BY ALAN ROBINSON

Older reef platforms provide a base for the next generation of living corals, including heads of smooth STAR CORAL.

is slow. Branches of elkhorn may lengthen only three or four inches each year; those of staghorn, six to eight inches annually. In linear dimension, the massive brain-coral heads are even slower: Heads of a foot or so in diameter may be fifty years old. It is understandable that the growth of the reef platform, many feet thick and composed of the remains of countless former colonies, requires thousands of years.

Natural processes of coral destruction are constantly at work upon the reef — from simple wave damage to the devastating effects of a hurricane, from the everyday feeding of parrotfishes to epidemics of disease or virtual plagues of predators such as certain starfish.

As the numbers of park visitors who snorkel and boat among St. John's reefs increase, accidental or deliberate visitor-related damage becomes a significant factor. Most damage is inadvertent and can usually be attributed to the novice snorkeler who lacks sufficient experience and self-confidence to relax in the water, to keep fins and elbows away from delicate formations, and to maneuver in shallow water. Indiscriminate anchoring by small boats can also become a serious

The growth forms of LETTUCE CORAL (Agaricia agaricites), like other corals, depend on environmental conditions. In shallow water it is a simple encrusting growth; at greater depths it is a fragile, leaf-like structure; in very dark water it occurs in broad horizontal plates with polyps present only on the upper sides.

destructive force, necessitating installation of permanent anchor buoys in some areas. Certain of the most heavily used reefs may eventually have to be closed to visitation to allow for regrowth; judging from the extremely slow growth rates, this could require many years.

A basic set of environmental conditions is required to sustain healthy growth of a reef. Sunlight and clear water are important, since the photosynthetic contribution of the zooxanthellae is critical. In general, reef growth in the world's oceans is limited to the tropics, where more sunlight is available year-round, and to shallow, well-lit depths of less than 150 feet. Since turbidity quickly reduces the quantity and quality of available light, and accumulations of silt can physically smother the polyps, reefs do not usually flourish in muddy bays or off turbid river mouths.

Dependable supplies of oxygen and planktonic food, and the cleansing action of water currents are also important. Reef growth is favored in high-energy surf and current zones such as off headlands and within well-flushed bays and channels.

Temperature and salinity requirements of corals are less easily explained; but, for physiological reasons relating to the animals' abilities to lay down calcium carbonate, optimum temperatures are found to be about 75 to 80 degrees. Optimum salinities are in the range of 30 to 36 parts per thousand (near the typical ocean value of 35 ppt).

Reefs or individual corals suffer when they are exposed to extremes of turbidity, temperature, salinity, or chemical pollution caused perhaps by a series of extremely low tides or extensive silt-laden or polluted freshwater runoff from the adjacent land. If exposure is prolonged, they eventually die.

The coral reefs of St. John are basically of two types: *fringing reefs*, found directly adjacent to the shore, usually with a recognizable attachment to the coastal rocks, and the deeper *patch reefs*, which occur at locations isolated from the shore or cut off from other reefs. In addition to these reef types (where living corals are growing on a carbonate base), individual coral colonies are commonly found in shallow water only a few feet offshore, growing directly on submerged coastal rocks and ledges.

Fire coral (Millepora complanata)

FIRE CORALS — which can cause an irritating rash when brushed — are not true hard corals. Although they do have carbonate skeletons, there are no distinct polyp cups; instead, the smooth surface is broken by thousands of tiny pores through which project thread-like tentacles bearing stinging cells. In shallow water, fire coral may form a simple, yellowish crust over rocks and dead corals, thus hastening the consolidation of a dying reef.

Fire coral (Millepora alcicornis)

The shallowest fringing reefs — like those at the eastern end of Cinnamon Bay, off Windswept Beach, and at Denis Bay — are easily approached by snorkelers on a calm day. These reefs are typically quite barren on their upper, wave-washed surfaces. At extreme low tides these surfaces may even be completely exposed. Within the many crevices lacing the top of the reef, hardy, encrusting sponges; mats of soft, yellowish colonial anemones (zooanthids); and short-spined red sea urchins *(Echinometra)* can be found. The outlines of dead coral colonies forming the reef tops are softened by attached seaweeds and encrusting forms of fire coral *(Millepora)*, which can deliver an irritating sting.

The first living hard-coral colonies are encountered along the seaward edge of typical fringing reefs. Sturdy, fan-shaped clumps of elkhorn coral *(Acropora palmata)*, often oriented in the direction of incoming waves, are interspersed with encrusting brain corals *(Diploria spp.)*, and fire coral in its finger-like growth form. The face of these reefs is steep, or even overhung, since the fastest coral growth is taking place on the upper part of the face. Delicate hard corals, such as lettuce *(Agaricia)* and tube coral *(Cladocora)*, survive well on this protected face. Nearer the base of the reef grow bulky hemispherical heads of brain and star corals *(Montastrea)*. During heavy seas the sand adjacent to the base of the reef frequently shifts, perhaps as much as two feet in depth, and the lowest heads on the reef are often damaged by abrasion or outright burial.

Various stages of shallow fringing reef development are apparent in the waters surrounding St. John. The minimum extent is that already

NPS PHOTO BY ALAN ROBINSON

Mennebec Bay, East End

Elkhorn (Acropora palmata)

NPS PHOTO BY ALAN ROBINSON

NPS PHOTO BY ALAN ROBINSON

ELKHORN CORAL dominates the shallow, high-wave energy zone on fringing reefs, where the typical branched form (upper left) is often broken by heavy surf. Colonies in deeper water (left) take on a graceful look, reaching upward to sunlit levels. Uncrowded conditions produce a fan-shaped growth (above).

Elkhorn coral, common on the shallow reefs (right), gives way to a related branching coral, STAGHORN (Acropora cervicornis), in areas where wave energies are lower. Loosely twined thickets of a deep-growing form (below) are found at the base of the fringing-reef face. Dense masses of short branches are characteristic in shallow waters, such as inside a protective reef barrier.

Staghorn coral, deep form

Staghorn coral, shallow form

Stoplight parrotfish

Many species of PARROTFISH, often in schools, roam over the shallow reefs. Their peculiar, beak-like teeth are the perfect tools for scraping the furry crust of algae from dead coral. Much of the sand on local reefs is a by-product of this method of feeding.

Queen parrotfish

Flamingo-tongue cowries on seawhip

Seaplume

GORGONIANS — seawhips, seaplumes, and seafans — are related to hard corals, but have flexible horny skeletons and only small amounts of carbonate, occurring as scattered spicules in the animal tissue. The polyps are small (lower left), and are interconnected by common channels. A gorgonian's flexible skeleton bends easily with the passing waves and currents — similarly shaped hard corals would break. A variety of small predators have evolved definite preferences for gorgonians.

Seawhip (Eunicea)

Seafan (Gorgonia flabellum)

Fireworm (Hermodice) on seafan

described for the reef at the eastern edge of Cinnamon Bay, where the reef crest has progressed only a few yards offshore. Off Annaberg, in the quieter waters of Mary Creek, the reef has extended seaward 100 yards or more. This extension has created a broad, back-reef flat only a few inches below low-tide level, where quite a different set of organisms find their niches. This includes a dense growth of the alga *Halimeda* (a green seaweed with a skeleton of calcium carbonate plates), and isolated patches of the warm-water-tolerant finger coral, *Porites porites*.

Over the many centuries in which the Mary Creek reefs have been developing, growth and destruction of these carbonate producers on the back-reef have resulted in sediment accumulating on the flats, filling in the interstices of the underlying coral rubble. This substrate supports a lush growth of the marine-adapted grass known as "turtle grass" (*Thalassia*).

A more mature reef profile is found at Lagoon Point, outside the boundaries of the park in Coral Bay. This reef is subject to continuous, moderate-to-heavy wave action, since it directly faces the open sea on the windward side of the island. A broad band of relatively fresh, jagged, coral frag-

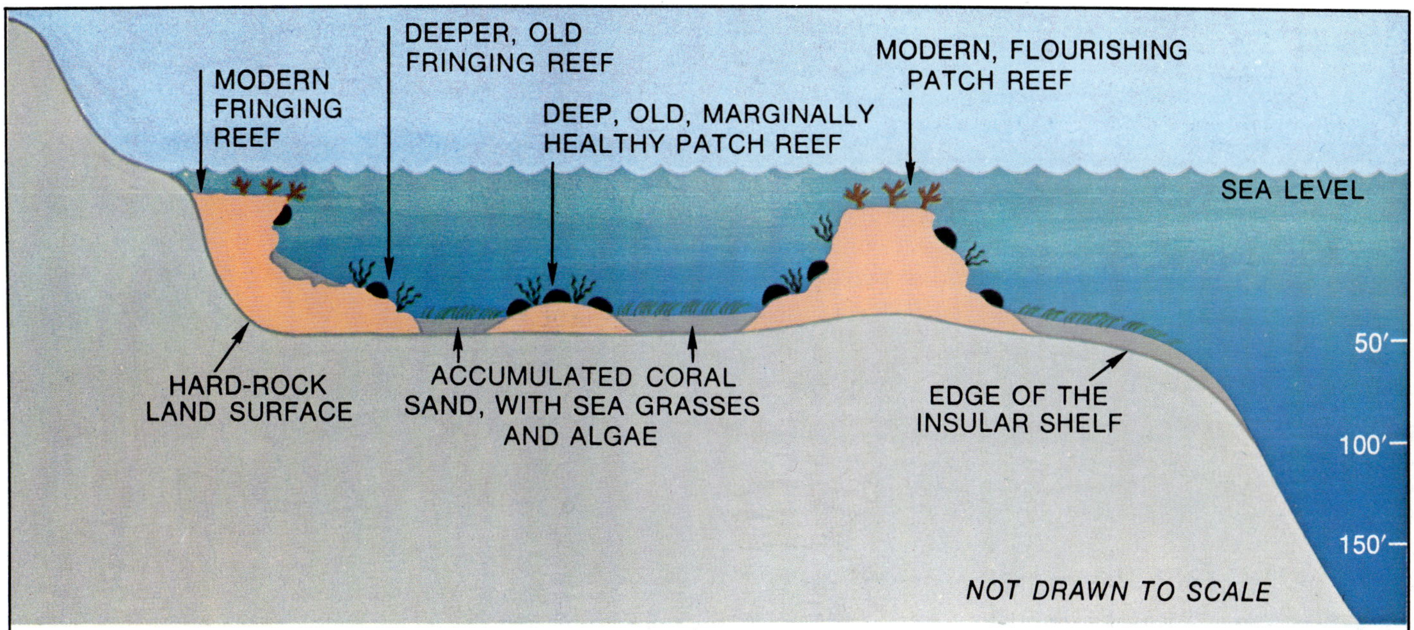

In this generalized profile of the insular shelf off St. John's north shore (see photo, pg. 15), the easily accessible reefs near shore are modern FRINGING REEFS, which drop off to an older fringing-reef system established during earlier (lower) sea levels. PATCH REEFS are scattered offshore, interspersed with accumulations of coral sand covered with seagrasses and algae. About fifteen miles north of St. John the shelf ends, dropping abruptly to depths of over 10,000 feet.

ments and coarse rubble lies immediately inshore of the reef crest. Shoreward lies a broad, shallow, productive lagoon, where sea grasses and algae exist in abundance alongside great raised beds of tightly packed finger coral.

Because of the windward exposure at Lagoon Point, large volumes of water are transported across the reef as waves constantly break on the seaward crest. Much of this flow enters the inshore lagoon and is eventually shunted off to either side in slightly deeper channels near the shore. Some of the flow is reflected from the reef crest itself and is funneled back to deeper water through a system of sand-floored grooves cutting through the sloping outer reef face. At Lagoon Point this "spur-and-groove" system is highly developed — an excellent example of similar phenomena found on reefs throughout the world.

An obvious but little appreciated effect of fringing reefs is that they provide a remarkably effective, self-repairing barrier between incoming waves and the shoreline. Without such a barrier, erosion of the adjacent coast would be taking place at a much faster rate, and the character of the coastal landscape of St. John would be radically different. The porous character of the reef allows it to absorb and dissipate great quantities of incoming energy, even that unleashed during the fury of a hurricane, thereby substantially reducing damage to the inner shore.

Fringing reefs have also played a role in the formation of the twenty-five or so saltponds in St. John. Although the sequence needs further documentation, it appears that reefs growing inward from opposing bay headlands eventually unite to form a continuous barrier across the bay mouth.

Brain coral thrown up on the beach by storms

This barrier is consolidated by the stirring of heavy wave action, and large amounts of coral rubble may be added during hurricanes. The barrier can then be colonized by hardy terrestrial vegetation, and sea water is eventually prevented from circulating in the bay. Subject to flooding and evaporation, the new pond becomes increasingly saline and the marine fauna is replaced by a characteristic high-salt-tolerant assemblage, often including dense populations of brine shrimp.

The saltpond plays an important role in the ecology of reefs: During heavy rains over the land, the ravines (locally termed "guts") flush out accumulations of sediment and debris. Typically this runoff drains into a saltpond; and, unless the pond has been filled or cut open by human activities, the flow is prevented from pouring out onto the nearshore reefs where the sediment or lowered salinity could have serious consequences. Following the flooding, the pond water slowly evaporates or filters through the barrier and flows out to the sea, having left its silt load as a harmless accumulation on the bottom of the pond.

Extensive evidence of a much older fringing-reef system is found in slightly deeper water off much of the coast. The reef stretching for several hundred yards parallel to the shoreline off Denis Bay, beginning in twenty-five to thirty feet of water, is a typical example.

These deeper reefs probably had their beginnings during a relatively long-lasting period of lower sea level. They are still active today, and usually have an upper, gently sloping basement of consolidated coral rock on which many gorgonians (sea fans and sea whips) and brain or star corals appear. Living coral outcrops are generally separated from each other by dead coral rubble covered by tough, furry algae, or by several inches of coarse sand and coral fragments.

Elkhorn coral, obviously the dominant species of hard coral in the shallow, high-energy zones, is conspicuously absent from the deeper fringing reefs. A closely related species called "staghorn" (*Acropora cervicornis*), a delicate and easily broken branching form, inhabits the deeper platforms, where its intertwined branches resemble a kind of undersea brush pile.

The face of the deeper fringing reef begins at about a twenty-five-foot depth; it then drops steeply to the sandy bottom at forty to fifty feet. Sometimes precipitous, the face, composed of loosely aggregated coral debris and living massive corals, is an impressive sight to the adventurous visitor who may leisurely inspect it with the aid

Along the windward (eastern) coasts of St. John, and especially at Buck Island, ELKHORN CORAL assumes a heavy, cylindrical form, providing added resistance to the constant pounding of waves blown in by the easterly tradewinds.

The whole of the park's northwest coastline and offshore area is covered in this remarkable aerial photograph. FRINGING REEFS are visible (adjacent to the shores at Hawksnest, Denis, Trunk, and Cinnamon bays). Extensive PATCH REEFS show as light (shallow) areas against a dark-blue (deeper) background. White streaks through the patch reefs are sand-floored SURGE CHANNELS oriented along the direction of prevailing waves.

of scuba equipment. Many of the larger species of common reef fishes are found here, including big-mouthed carnivorous groupers; ghostly, platter-sized angel-fish; and secretive heavy-bodied moray eels. The deep crevices and overhanging ledges are typical daytime dens for the Caribbean spiny lobster *(Panulirus argus)* and its darker cousin, the spotted rock lobster *(Panulirus guttatus)*, who has the peculiar habit of clinging upside down in its protected den.

A lucky diver may encounter a sleepy young hawksbill or green sea turtle wedged under a ledge, resting after a feeding excursion on a nearby grass bed. Sometimes a grey, heavy-bodied nurse shark can be seen slowly cruising along the sand near the reef or tucked far back under an overhang. These relatively benign creatures rarely express much interest in a diver (unless provoked). Chances of encountering any of the more agressive, open-water species of shark on St. John's inshore reefs are rather small. Fortunately, since spearfishing in any form is prohibited, divers within park waters do not tempt these predators with struggling, wounded fish.

Patch reefs (also termed *bank reefs*) are composed more or less of the same species of corals found on fringing reefs, but they differ from the latter in that they are separated from the land and are surrounded by a non-reef habitat. These isolated patch reefs probably represent regions of continuous reef-building dating back to earlier, shallower sea levels. As the water rose, reef growth and the accumulation of foundation material kept pace, resulting in coral-capped mounds

Sailboat running downwind off Turtle Bay

rising in sharp relief from the flat surrounding shelf.

The steep-sided patch reefs have an appearance similar to the deeper fringing reefs already described, with near-vertical slopes composed of living and dead massive corals rising from forty- to sixty-foot depths. Some patch reefs, such as Johnson Reef off Trunk Bay, slope more gently — indicating they were probably built upon hard rock rising from the underlying shelf and therefore do not represent a continuous accumulation of coral.

NATIONAL OCEAN SURVEY

Maho Bay

Edge of the Sea: Sand and Surf

The sandy beaches of St. John are certainly the most visible and the most popular resource of the park; yet many visitors lack an understanding and appreciation of the processes which create and maintain them.

The existence and form of any beach depend on the interaction between the energy of incoming waves and currents and the type of material available on that particular shore. Within the park's ten miles of shoreline the full spectrum of that interaction can be found.

In bays with shallow offshore waters and strategically placed reefs, gently sloping expanses of fine, nearly pure coral sand are found. Off straighter, steeper coastal sections — where wave energies are higher on the beach, and the reef growth is in deeper water — there may be a steep, rough, porous beach composed entirely of battered pieces of coral or smoothly rounded cobbles derived from the breakdown of rocks from the surrounding shore. Off the very steepest headlands and cliffs exposed to frequent heavy seas, only the heaviest, most angular boulders remain in place.

Despite such generalizations, the critical factors which determine beach form in a given locale cannot be understood without a thorough analysis of offshore bottom topography, reef condition, and "energy dynamics"—wave height, angle of approach, tidal currents, and storm frequency. All of these conditions can vary significantly over distances of just a few hundred feet. For instance, the beaches in three adjacent bays at Lameshur, on the park's southeast shore, are all radically different in form: Europa Bay is pure coral rubble; Little Lameshur is a fine-sand beach; Greater Lameshur is a 200-yard stretch of beautifully rounded cobblestones.

As new carbonate material is constantly being generated, rearranged, and broken down on the reef, large quantities of particulate debris are formed. This debris ranges from the daily production of sand-sized particles passing through the intestines of a thousand grazing parrotfishes to great chunks of coral rock occasionally torn loose by storm waves. Hard parts from other reef associates — skeletons of the calcareous algae, broken mollusk shells, and sea-urchin spines — add substantially to this growing layer of sand, which is continuously moved off the reef by waves and currents into a surrounding sand reserve.

These reserves, supplemented by only minor amounts of terrestrial rocks weathered down to fine particles, are the major, and most critical, source of sand for St. John's renowned beaches. No great rivers flow down from the land bringing loads of sand and gravel to these beaches; no unending supply drifts mysteriously in from some vast stockpile. The key to the existence of the coral sand beach is the living reef.

The principal force shifting sand from the reefs to the shore is wave action; a surprising amount of this movement takes place during relatively infrequent periods of high-energy, storm-wave conditions.

St. John's north shore is subject annually to to heavy winter "ground seas"—actually large, evenly spaced swells created by storms in the central Atlantic occurring perhaps 2,000 miles distant. As many as twenty times from October to April, waves up to eight feet high may suddenly build up out of the north, crashing on exposed beaches and creating turbid, grayish water and strong, near-shore currents capable of moving large quantities of sand. During the three to five days in which such swells continue to arrive, sea level on the northern shore is temporarily elevated. During this "storm surge," normal high tides (actually rather small in range — about a foot) may go a foot or more above normal, sending the breaking waves even higher on the beach, sometimes overwashing through the line of vegetation.

The limit to the depth at which these big waves can effectively move sediment is about twenty-five feet, except under hurricane conditions. Thus the material produced on the deeper reefs, or sand which has been transported to deeper water (in phenomena similar to landslides or slumping on land), is removed from the beach supply system. Additional losses occur at the beach itself when sand is blown inland, is overwashed, or is ground down to very fine material swept from the beach by wave backwash and held in suspension long enough to be carried offshore by currents. To offset these losses the system must be constantly resupplied by the production of the living shallow reefs.

NPS PHOTO BY SCOTT HOFFMAN

Ground sea breaking at Cinnamon Bay

It is very difficult to make an objective measure of the rate at which St. John's reefs supply sand to her shores. But it is known that local beaches are slow to recover from the effects of artificial withdrawals of material, such as the mining of sand directly off the beach face or the dredging and removal of sand from a shallow sand reserve offshore.

Considerable sand was in fact removed from beaches in St. Thomas and St. John for use as

Mature fringing reef with inshore lagoon at Lagoon Point, Coral Bay (outside park boundaries)

Century plant (Agave) in full bloom

construction material. This was done at a time when the full implications of this practice were not yet known. It will be many years — perhaps hundreds — before these beaches regain a full complement of sand. Along a rugged coastline like that of St. John, headlands seem to prevent much lateral transfer of sand from bay to bay, effectively turning individual bays into relatively closed boxes in terms of sand reserves.

Besides acting as a sand-supply source and as a direct barrier to incoming waves, reefs may have indirect effects on wave energy. Over a long term the development of a shallow reef may result in subtle but consistent changes in the direction in which the incoming waves travel (by refraction). The angle at which waves arrive has a great influence upon the form of a beach and especially on the strength of lateral currents set up directly off the beach face — currents responsible for moving sand along the shore.

The energy barrier protection provided by a reef is dramatically demonstrated in the wake of some catastrophic event, such as a hurricane, when whole sections of a reef crest may be destroyed. Beaches previously in balance when wave energy filtered through the reef are now open to a more direct wave attack. The new balance struck may involve considerable change in both the form and content of the beach — probably from a gently sloping, fine-sand beach to one which rises more steeply and is composed of predominantly coarse material. In an extreme example, the sand may be stripped away completely, leaving either the underlying bedrock or a layer of cobbles.

Because the necessary growing conditions for coral will likely be re-established, hurricane damage — though sudden and devastating — is generally followed by regrowth of the reef. But when a reef is killed by a continuing source of pollution from municipal or industrial wastes or by the turbidity and disruption following a dredging, the effects on an adjacent beach are long lasting. The energy shield has been removed, and so has the source of the sand.

Coral sand beaches offer a limited but critical biological habitat for certain species, notably the sea turtles. Though increasingly rare throughout the tropical seas, green and hawksbill turtles are still commonly seen in St. John's inshore waters, and traditionally a few adult females use park beaches as nesting sites during June through Sep-

As the fringing reef at Annaberg matures, the inshore flats slowly fill with sand.

Dry forest and cactus vegetation on the windward shore, Ram Head and Salt Pond Bay

tember. Unlike the few remaining mass nesting beaches around the Caribbean, where many hundreds of animals will struggle ashore in a single evening, St. John's records are usually of isolated females totaling only a dozen or so nesting forays annually. In the early 1960's the park participated in the release of several hundred hatchling green turtles airlifted to St. John from a traditional mass nesting beach in Costa Rica. It is not known what effect these releases may have had on sustaining the local green-turtle population (since it is impossible to successfully tag the hatchlings), but it is hoped that at least a few of those which survived to adulthood are returning to St. John's beaches to nest.

The HAWKSBILL SEA TURTLE, like most species of the world's heavily exploited marine turtles, has been declared endangered.

Leatherback turtles, a gigantic species changed little from its forebears eons ago, still nest on some beaches in the Virgin Islands. Some specimens may attain a length of eight feet and weight of 1,000 pounds. Another name for this species is "trunkback," which is one possible explanation of the origin of the name *Trunk Bay.*

The moist sand of the upper beach after a rainfall or an especially high tide is also a prime breeding site for an organism at the opposite end of the size spectrum — the irritating sand fly. Sand flies (technically not flies, but biting midges of the insect family *Ceratapogonidae)* also breed in other damp habitats, such as among stones on a cobble beach, along swamp edges and the fluctuating shoreline of saltponds.

The physical environment within the surf zone of a sandy beach, where the sand is constantly being shifted, battered and rearranged, is a severe one. But a few hardy organisms do exist there, such as the white ghost crab. This excellently camouflaged two-inch side-stepper makes its burrow at the high-tide line and feeds by scampering

Fortsberg Hill, Coral Harbor, and the flat land of Estate Carolina adjoin the earliest settlement on St. John.

about above the wave swash, where decaying seagrass and other organic debris are available. Further down the beach, below the tide level, lives a small species of swimming crab. Its ability to bury itself in the sand in a few seconds saves it from being swept away (and from being eaten by a predator).

A wide variety of bivalve (clam-like) mollusks is known to inhabit the lower beach face and the shallow, sandy bottom immediately offshore, where wave turbulence brings adequate food to these filter-feeders. But, curiously, few of St. John's beaches offer very good "shelling" to collectors. Perhaps the rather slight tidal range (about a foot) and the extremely gentle surf during most of the year do not generally provide sufficient energy to bring these mollusks up onto the beach.

Several species of fish commonly venture into the surf zone to feed on unwary crabs or mollusks temporarily exposed by the breaking waves. The graceful little black-finned, silver "palometo" is frequently encountered darting about a swimmer's feet as the disturbed upper layers of sand reveal potential food items.

Beginning just outside the active surf zone off most of the island's sandy beaches (such as Caneel) is an expanse of coarse, clean, remarkably irregular sand. Here tube-building worms, large bivalves, and the burrowing ghost shrimp are responsible for an impressive array of mounds, hummocks, cones, and depressions. These inshore sandy areas are in a sense mere continuations of the beach — material here is the first to be shifted on or offshore during periods of heavy waves. The organisms which make their homes here must be particularly tolerant of an occasional uprooting.

A bit deeper, in one of the most mysterious scenes awaiting a snorkeler or diver, lie fields of graceful bottom-dwelling garden eels. These harm-

Broad-bladed TURTLE GRASS, finer MANATEE GRASS, and a stalked green alga known as NEPTUNE'S SHAVING BRUSH are present on an undersea grassland.

less, three-foot relatives of the powerful moray make their homes in deep burrows in the sand, extending their swaying, snake-like bodies partly out of their holes to take delicate snaps at passing plankton. Wary beasts, they quickly disappear into the sand, tail first, at the slightest hint of a disturbance.

UNDERSEA GRASSLANDS

The seagrass beds which cover large expanses of the bottom off St. John between the coral reefs are composed of several different species of remarkably adapted relatives of common terrestrial grasses. Turtle and manatee grasses are actually proper green plants (not algae), with stems, leaves, roots, and an inter-connecting system of rhizomes. These tough underground stems serve to weave adjacent plants together into a mat firm enough to resist scouring by wave action.

The seagrass stabilizes the substrate and, by slowing down the currents just above the bottom, encourages fine material to settle out of the water. Material thus trapped is less easily brought back into suspension during rough weather — an important factor in maintaining good water quality for reef growth. This stabilizing function is eliminated when near-shore dredging operations strip away the grass to get at and remove the cleaner sand below. Following bottom abuse in a dredging, water which is highly turbid due to suspension of fine materials may continue for months, with serious consequences on nearby reefs.

Healthy seagrass meadows contribute large expanses of food-rich habitat for a number of animals, including some specially adapted stony corals which do not require a hard substrate for attachment. The small, solitary cup coral *Manicina* is one of these. It has solved the problem of being

The LONGSPINED BLACK SEA URCHIN (Diadema, locally known as "sea egg") can be a hazard to swimmers.

The Island

Evidence supporting theories of drifting continents and a widening ocean floor has increased recently with advances in deep-ocean drilling and other modern techniques of probing the sea floor. It seems to be a well-accepted theory that North and South America were once fused in a great primordial land mass with what is now Europe and Africa. The great basin which now separates the New World from the Old — the Atlantic Ocean — formed gradually over the past 200

INTRUSIONS and metamorphic changes in older rocks are typical at Mary Point and Whistling Cay.

million years as these massive continental plates slowly drifted apart.

The Caribbean basin itself appears to be underlain by a separate, smaller plate. The trenches, deeps, and volcanic islands fringing the basin are understood to be areas of great stress where there is continued interaction between the Caribbean and Atlantic plates. This is particularly evident along the eastern boundary of the Caribbean, where active volcanism in the Lesser Antilles attests to the tremendous heat still being generated in the crust as the spreading Atlantic floor is driven slowly downward beneath the Caribbean plate.

Within the Greater Antilles, which form the northern boundary of the basin — Cuba, Jamaica, Hispaniola, Puerto Rico and the Virgin Islands, great east-to-west fault systems are evident as the plate forming the North American continent grinds haltingly away from the slower-moving Caribbean block. Puerto Rico and the northern Virgin Islands, St. John included, lie along this fault system, and the geologic history of these islands is predominantly one of volcanism, faulting, and major uplift.

In St. Thomas and St. John a relatively clear geologic record stretches back some 100 million years to the late Cretaceous period. This places the earliest stages of island-building at a time when the major continents were probably much closer together. Important clues to the history of the Caribbean basin and its evolution may yet be discovered in the record of rocks exposed in these islands.

A FIERY HISTORY

The first events in the development of St. Thomas and St. John took place as a series of volcanic flows erupted slowly onto a deep ocean floor and solidified. These layers, subsequently uplifted, are still recognizable as separate flows, and are the oldest exposed rocks on St. John. They are collectively known as the *Water Island* formation.

THE MAJOR BEACHES on St. John are located along the park's northwestern coast. The Mary Point peninsula and islands to the north make this a leeward (wind-protected) shore; coral sand from offshore reefs is the source of supply. Explosively-cooled volcanic rocks underlie much of the north shore.

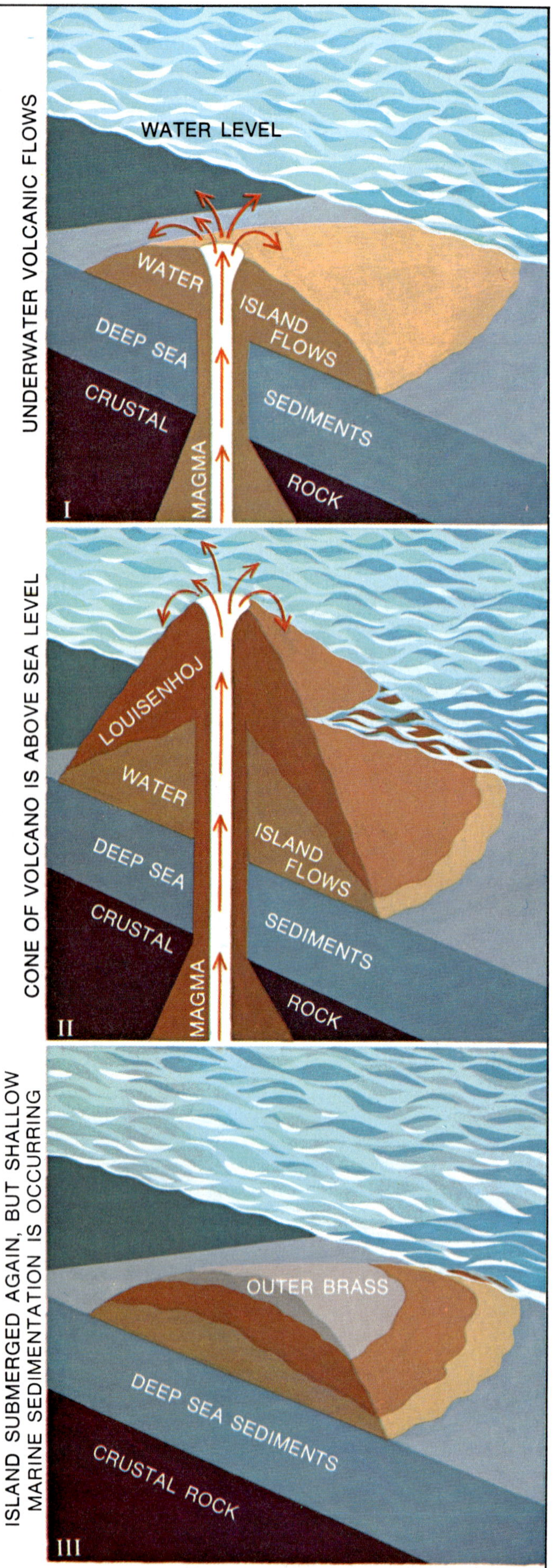

St. John's geologic history combines a period of ancient submarine volcanic flows (I), followed by explosive above-water volcanism (II), and later organic deposition of marine sediments (III).

These rocks were evidently formed underwater at great depths, since there is little evidence of pumice or explosive fragmentation in the early part of the sequence. A water depth of some 15,000 feet would be required to create the tremendous pressure necessary to keep the molten rock from cooling explosively. Further evidence has come from a very deep drill hole at Ram Head on St. John — a drilling which succeeded in penetrating more than 2,000 feet of Water Island rock. Beneath this volcanic material lies a soft, sticky clay similar to sediments found elsewhere only on the deep ocean floor.

As these early flows were thickening and solidifying over a period of perhaps millions of years, the depth of water over the newly formed rock decreased. This was probably accompanied by a generalized uplifting of the whole area as stresses began building in the crust during continental drift.

The next period of rock development in St. John was a time of explosive shallow water and subaerial (above-water) volcanism. The resulting material, the *Louisenhoj* (Louise-en-hoi) formation, contains extensive explosive volcanic products such as andesite and tuff (solidified ash), and even cobbles and fragments of the older Water Island rock. The violence of this period is evidenced by the huge boulders of the older Water Island which were thrown up and still lie scattered on St. John's hillsides.

The thickness and appearance of the Louisenhoj in St. John and St. Thomas indicate the volcanic center was under what is presently known as Pillsbury Sound, the shallow channel now separating the two sister islands. Over the many thousands of years that subaerial volcanic activity occurred, the material on the slopes of the resulting cone was extensively weathered and was eventually redeposited as relatively fine-grained rock in the shallow surrounding seas.

Most of the modern island of St. John is composed of the older volcanic formations. The distinctive dark-blue-to-grey flows of the Water Island rock make up the entire southeastern half of St. John, including East End. This material forms the rugged promontories of the park's eastern and southern coasts.

The northwestern section of St. John, closer to the site of the presumed ancient volcano, is formed predominantly of the younger Louisenhoj rocks, ranging in color from light green to dark blue. Older exposed material has weathered and become reddish. The gentler, more subdued north-

judging from
throughout t
the Virgin I
occurred, wh
period long
to build up
terraces has
100 feet off
have off man

There is
stand terrac
above mode
indicate that
but rather t
uplift which
elevation.

During t
period of g
fluctuating
level occurre
reefs eviden
deepening w
a foundation
of reefs disc
veys out on
keep up wit
"drowned."
rently being
sandy mater

The lack
Thomas and
the recent s

ern coastline from Cruz Bay to Francis Bay lies within this formation. Numerous small "pocket" beaches of rounded dark-blue cobbles have given rise to the local name of the Louisenhoj rock — "Blue Beach."

The close of the fiery second phase of St. John's development was followed by a period of relative serenity during which organically derived sediments (from corals and the skeletons of planktonic creatures) slowly accumulated on the slopes of the emerging island. The first layer over the older volcanics is a dark-colored limestone known as the *Outer Brass,* named after a small island north of St. Thomas where it is well exposed. This thin-bedded limestone was deposited over many thousands of years by a continuous rain of the skeletons of planktonic algae to the ocean floor in shallow, fertile seas. Only a few hundred feet thick, the Outer Brass formation has been tilted considerably and has only a limited exposure on St. John — in the area of Mary Creek.

The Outer Brass limestone is overlain by a much more substantial formation of relatively impure sediments *(wackes)* composed of debris of the Louisenhoj and Outer Brass. This *Tutu*

Waves pound on the windward (east-facing) coastlines unprotected by reefs. At Nanny Point, flows of WATER ISLAND ROCK are exposed, essentially unaltered since their origins 100 million years ago. EASTER ROCK, at Hawksnest, is a rounded fragment of the same rock tossed out of place during later volcanism.

Buck Island Reef National Monument

The third (and largest) of the U. S. Virgin Islands is St. Croix, forty miles south of St. John. In 1961 a presidential proclamation set aside 850 acres of the landscape and reefs of Buck Island, a uniquely beautiful, mile-long volcanic islet off the northeast tip of St. Croix, as Buck Island Reef National Monument.

Used for many years as a goat pasture — hence the name "Buck" Island — the island's steep slopes and spectacular near-shore reefs had already achieved distinction as the first territorial park (1948). It has had a long history of aesthetic appreciation by Virgin Islanders.

The island has no human residents nor camping facilities, but visitors traditionally arrive for a day of swimming, snorkeling, or trail-walking aboard small sail- or motor-charters out of Christiansted, St. Croix.

The spotted drum (Equetus punctatus) is one of many reef organisms capable of producing underwater sound. Assorted snaps, pops, grunts, and scraping noises create a continuous background symphony on the reef.

Underwater Photography
by Clarendon Bowman

A break in the reef front on the northeast shore

The magnificent reef stretching like a barrier 2,000 yards along the eastern half of Buck Island probably originated as a simple fringing reef. Rising sea levels raised the reef crest while strong currents and streaming sand kept the inshore lagoon free of coral.

Red-spined urchin on star coral

Spotted scorpionfish

Nassau grouper

Spotted trunkfish

Over 300 species of marine fish from the Caribbean are known. Each fills a role in daily (and nightly) reef affairs, such as these predatory groupers, nocturnal crab-eating squirrelfishes, and algae-grazing surgeonfishes. Some parrotfishes secrete a mucous sleeping sac at night, which may help to hide their scent from predators.

Parrotfish asleep in mucous sac

Squirrelfish

Surgeonfish: blue tang

Good visibility in tropical waters may explain the evolution of bright color patterns for sexual recognition among fishes, such as the YELLOWTAIL SNAPPER.

Most primitive of the multicellular animals on the reef, SPONGES remain attached to the substrate. They depend on water currents to bring fine plankton food near enough to be sucked into thousands of tiny pores lined by beating cilia. Often unpalatable to predators, the colorful sponges come in all shapes, ranging from simple encrusting mats to great baskets and tubes.

Tube sponge (Agelis)

Vase sponge (Callyspongia)

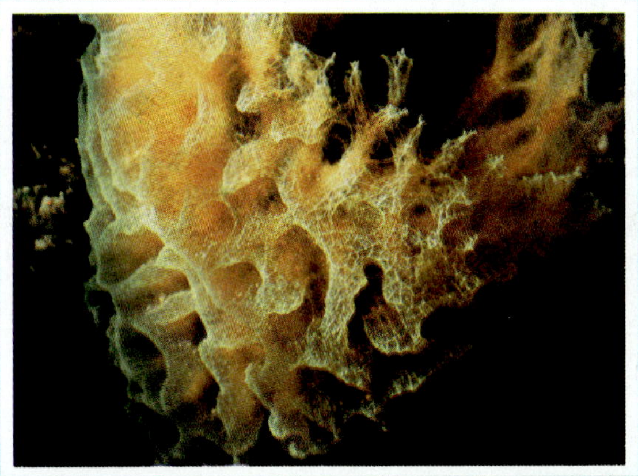

Vase sponge detail

Representing ancient relatives of modern starfish, this flexible, many-armed CRINOID lives tucked into crevices on the Buck Island reef. Usually attached by its central, root-like pedestal (white), it is capable of slow-motion moves to better filter-feeding locales.

Basic similarities exist between the individual polyps of HARD CORALS (below) and SEA ANEMONES (left) which have no internal carbonate skeleton. Great mats of this colonial green anemone cover parts of the protected inshore side of the barrier reef.

Colonial anemone (Zooanthus)

Coral (Eusmilia)

Smooth trunkfish

Plume worms: These feathery filter-feeders can retract instantly into their coral-encased tubes.

Dozens of species of crab- and shrimp-like crustaceans fit into the economy of the reef. This ARROW CRAB keeps his spindly legs hidden from marauding fishes while delicately plucking a lunch of algae.

The CARIBBEAN SPINY LOBSTER lacks the massive claws of his northern relative. Living in reef crevices during the day, he ventures out nightly to feed on mollusks in adjacent grasslands. The size of local populations may be limited by the scarcity of mangrove lagoons, where juvenile lobsters must seek shelter.

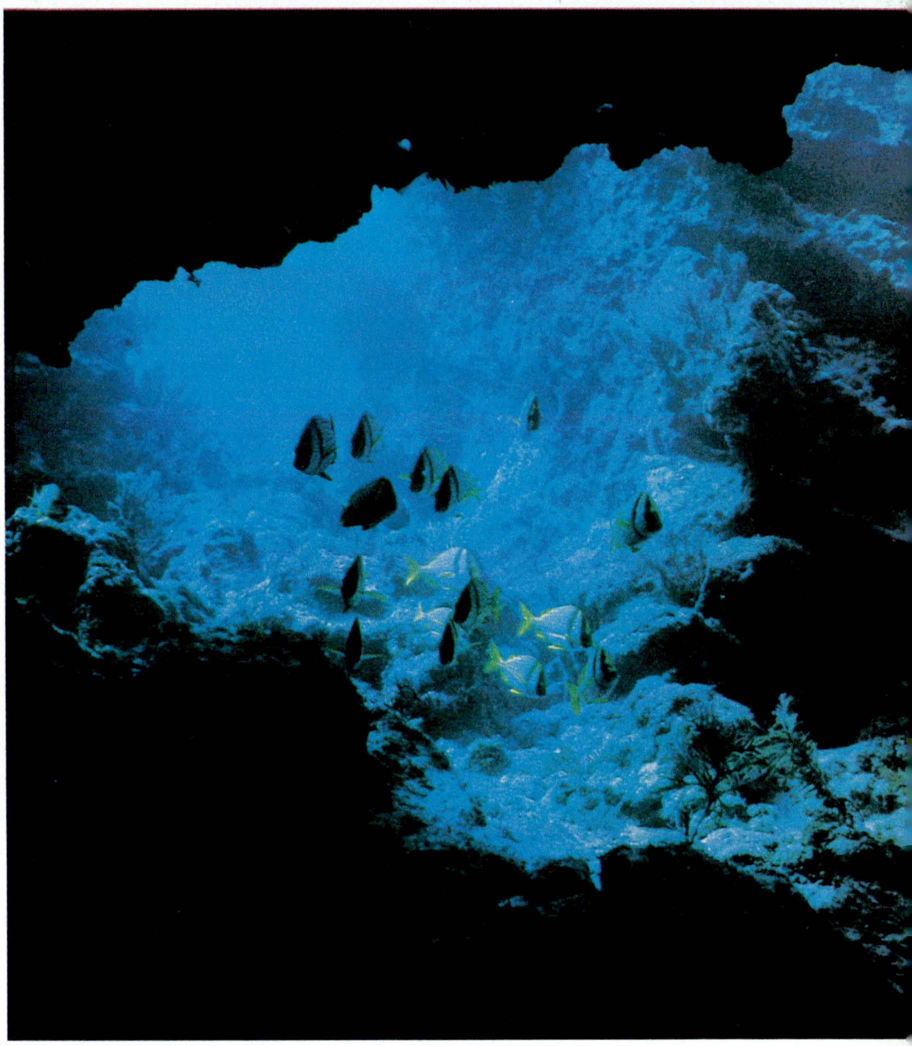

St. John: Yesterday and Today

St. John, like most of its Caribbean island neighbors, supported a small population of coastal-dwelling Indians of South American origin, the *Arawaks,* prior to European discovery in the 1490's.

Forerunners of the Arawaks, living on the coasts of Venezuela and Guyana, had been forced by aggressive competitors to migrate to offshore islands. In stepwise fashion, showing increasing skills, bands of these traditionally "forest" people progressed northward up the string of the Lesser Antilles arc, reaching St. John perhaps as early as 300 A.D. Then, as now, winds and currents would favor such a migration. In many cases the next northward island (or some evidence of it — such as a stationary cloud pattern) is actually visible from the island of departure.

Although the larger islands with their abundant flat coastal lands or higher rainfall were favored for settlement by the pioneer Arawaks, some sites on St. John were apparently suitable for extended periods of occupation by small groups. Principal dwelling sites have been discovered on the north and northwest coasts of the island (Cinnamon, Turtle, Caneel, and Cruz Bay) where slightly higher rainfall and more protection from hurricane winds would have offered better conditions than on the southern shores. Short-term campsites, occupied only during fishing and collecting expeditions, have been found in several other locations (Lameshur, Haulover) on the arid, windswept southeastern coasts where even subsistence farming would seem unlikely.

Where rainfall and soil permitted, the Arawak groups practiced simple slash-and-burn agriculture with manioc (brought with them) as the principal crop. Fish, shellfish and an occasional sea turtle, along with forest- and shore-bird species, supplied needed protein. It is possible that the Arawaks brought with them the "hutia" *(Isolobodon),* a traditional food source available to their forebears in South America. This large rodent cannot be found today on any of the Virgin Islands, yet its bones have often been discovered associated with St. John dwelling sites.

Two other land animals, the common iguana and a South American red-legged tortoise, may also have been first brought to the Virgin Islands tucked away in the ocean-going canoes of the Arawaks. These animals are still present on St. John but are very rarely seen.

Arawak peoples (perhaps representing two or more distinct migrations from the south) apparently existed in frugal harmony with the island's resources for about 1,000 years. They seem to have been displaced by yet another northward-extending tribe — the aggressive, cannibalistic *Caribs.* Historical reports originating with early

Since 1726 this MORAVIAN CHURCH has stood in the village of Emmaus in Coral Bay, where the first formal settlement of St. John by Europeans and Africans took place in 1716. Periodically battered by human events and hurricanes — it was virtually destroyed in 1916 — the building and the faith it represents have provided strong social continuity to generations of St. Johnians.

European visitors indicate these Indians spread northward through the Lesser Antilles only a century or so before Columbus first contacted them in his earliest voyages. The Spaniards actually encountered and skirmished with Caribs in St. Croix in 1493, yet there is no historical record of the presence of either the Caribs or the Arawaks in St. John at that time. Significantly, no European-produced artifacts have ever been discovered within an Arawak site on St. John. This lack suggests that these people had been driven from the island by Caribs or by drought before any significant contact with the Old World was established.

NPS PHOTO

Enigmatic PETROGLYPHS above a pool in the Reef Bay valley may be of Indian or African slave origin.

THE SUGAR YEARS

In the period between the first European discovery of the northern Virgin Islands by Columbus on his second voyage in 1493 and formal settlement some 200 years later, St. John had few recorded visitors. Occasional conflicting claims were made upon the island by Danish, Dutch, English, and even Spanish interests. Although Denmark did not legally establish sovereignty until much later (1754), St. Thomas was formally settled in 1672 by agents of the private, but chartered, Danish West India and Guinea Company.

In 1694 the company finally acted to take formal possession of St. John, but it was some twenty years later (1716) that the first company-operated plantation was established on the island at Estate Carolina in Coral Bay.

Several other estates had already been established on St. John by independent planters from St. Thomas or Tortola (in the British Virgin Islands). Exercising its charter rights, the company set about implementing procedures by which the independents were encouraged to continue their plantations, eventually becoming subject to company taxation. Tax-free status was granted for the first eight years, but with a stiff proviso that to gain clear title to sugar-producing land a mill and a sugar factory had to be constructed on the plantation by the end of that time.

Although wealthy estate owners did complete the prodigious clearing and construction needed to satisfy the company's demand, many settlers then and later chose instead to raise cotton. Although cotton was less suited than sugar to the islands and yielded a lesser profit, its production required a considerably smaller investment in processing equipment.

It was a simple economic fact, however, that neither sugar nor cotton could have been successfully grown in these early years without the labor provided by plantation slaves. The "unfree," as the predominantly West African blacks and their descendents were termed, consistently outnumbered the Europeans on St. John after agriculture was established. An abortive revolt by a segment of St. John's plantation slaves occurred in 1733, but slavery as a social order existed on the island and throughout the Danish West Indies until 1848, when emancipation was proclaimed by the Danish governor in the face of the rising likelihood of major revolt.

Emancipation and the resultant loss of free labor rapidly brought to a close the initial sugar and cotton estate days, which extended from about 1690 to 1850. St. John's population, which in the most active plantation period may have numbered about 2,000 (slaves all but 100 or so), fell to nearly 700, a figure maintained, more or less, up until the 1950's.

Only scattered garden plots of SUGAR CANE remain where great plantations once flourished.

NPS PHOTO BY ALAN ROBINSON

The Annaberg Ruins

Some eighty different cotton and sugar plantations have existed on St. John over the years. The windmill and boiling house at Annaberg were constructed in several phases; the most recent was an unsuccessful attempt in the late 1800's to reestablish the plantation after the slaves were emancipated. Partially reconstructed by the Park Service in the 1960's, Annaberg is used in living-history demonstrations of the daily activities of plantation workers. (See inside front cover for another view of Annaberg.)

Interest in sugar culture was temporarily revived after 1875, when a more profitable variety of cane was introduced. Some of the earlier estates were rebuilt on a much larger scale. At Reef Bay, steam power was added to the cane-crushing process to avoid the uncertainties of animal or wind power. But by the early 1900's competition from mainland-grown beet sugar, labor costs, and the depleted soil left by earlier agricultural practices combined to call the final halt to sugar's history in St. John.

Extensive grazing of cattle, goats, horses, and mules for export to St. Thomas and Puerto Rico continued on the land once used for cane. Many of the island's residents assumed a simple but self-sufficient life style centered around fishing and the farming of crops such as bananas, limes, coconuts, sugar apples, and mangoes.

The production of bay oil, an aromatic essence used in perfumes, provided additional income for a few of St. John's native families until the 1930's. An overgrown but still stately grove of the smooth-barked bay trees whose leaves yield the oil still stands on the moist and shady slopes of Bordeaux Mountain. From these slopes one can still follow the steep trails which once rang with the hooves of donkeys laden with bulging sackfuls of pungent leaves destined for the copper bay-oil stills of estates Lameshur and Carolina.

THE ENCROACHING FOREST

Two hundred and fifty years of intensive agriculture on St. John's meager flatlands and steep slopes have had considerable impact on the land and vegetation. Cane, cotton, and lesser amounts of indigo, tobacco, and other cash crops were grown virtually anywhere the land was not too rocky or too steep to stand on. Although production may have been encouraging in the first decades, erosion brought on by land clearing eventually removed much of the sparse topsoil, flushing it to the lowlands and thence to the sea. In the short-lived second phase of sugar culture, extensive terracing attempted to hold the remaining soil, but the ground had already lost much of its ability to retain moisture, and rainfall runoff was faster and more destructive than before.

All of the modern forest vegetation of St. John is second or third growth, and bears only partial resemblance to the virgin forest of the 1500's. However, since the island was not totally cleared at any one time, many of the original forest species have survived.

Only a few of the forest trees were cut for timber, but *Lignum vitae*, whose incredibly dense wood was in great demand for production of gears and pulleys in eighteenth-and nineteenth-century industrialization and ship-building, was almost completely eliminated in its wild state in the Virgin Islands.

Even the land unsuited to plantations was not spared. Selective tree clearing on St. John was practiced for over 200 years in the process of making charcoal. Charcoal for domestic use was exported to St. Thomas and St. Croix for many years, and its use on St. John was widespread until very recent times. On any of the trails cross-

Some introduced tree species are especially cherished by St. Johnians. The South American GENIP (left) produces a pleasantly tart, large-seeded fruit in late summer. The Old World TAMARIND (right) may provide a hundred years of shade. It constantly rains seed pods, which can be brewed into tea.

ing the park the hiker may see dark-stained circles of earth where a charcoal cutter labored for weeks or months, moving on only when the forest around him was laid quite bare.

Perhaps half the common forest trees now on St. John are species introduced after land clearing first began. Certain of the exotic (introduced) trees, such as the wild tamarind, have a distinct competitive advantage over native species because of altered soil and water conditions. Although there is no virgin forest on St. John — or anywhere in the U.S. or British Virgin Islands — the steep slopes of the upper valleys of Reef and Fish bays support a mature growth resembling the virgin condition. Here the upper canopy extends to forty feet or so, indicating that many of the trees escaped cutting when these valleys were put back into cane production in the late 1800's.

The characteristic wind-flattened scrub and low barrel-cactus vegetation on arid exposed points such as Ram Head are probably quite similar in general appearance to the flora of 300 years ago. Yet even these barren promontories have been subject to persistent grazing by goats, and it is not yet known which plant species may have been exterminated or suppressed.

Tree cactus

Calabash tree

NPS PHOTO BY ALAN ROBINSON

Turk's cap cactus

Turpentine tree (gumbo limbo)

Vegetation native to St. John

IN THE YEARS following the collapse of sugar production, much of St. John's land was used for grazing. This private, beautifully tended "grass piece" at Estate Susannaberg is on one of the last such farms on the island. A mixed orchard of soursops, sugar apples, guavas, and lime trees adds richness to the land.

The large majority of the island's southern slopes, particularly those just recovering from cattle and domestic stock grazing, are presently dominated by a jumbled, thorny, and literally impenetrable assemblage of exotic and native trees and shrubs. But less than twenty years ago these same slopes were virtually treeless expanses of broad-bladed, yellow-green guinea grass, itself a relative newcomer to the Caribbean from West Africa.

An added element in St. John's vegetational history is that of progressive climatic change. Although accurate records do not exist for the early sugar era, it is clear that during the more recent past (1912 onward) the Virgin Islands have received progressively less rainfall. For the period 1852-1911, average annual rainfall in the Virgin Islands was about 47 inches, whereas from 1912-1961 the annual average was near 44 inches. This difference may seem small, but even a 6% decline in average rainfall would have an impact on the groundwater storage and stream flow, and also on the character of the vegetation which is redeveloping within the park's protected boundaries.

Park managers on St. John (as in other parklands) are now facing the question of what steps to take, if any, to encourage a return to vegetative types similar to those existing before European intervention. Virgin Islands National Park is in fact designated a *natural area* park, and by general policy such parks are to be managed "back" toward the pristine condition. Yet also at issue is the wider philosophical dilemma as to whether or not land clearing and its consequences on St. John were themselves valid evolutionary processes. This is a complex question, and perhaps only academic, since major unmanageable factors affecting forest conditions and growth — soil, water, and climate — may be substantially different now than in pre-Columbian times.

A young RED MANGROVE tree takes hold on the edge of the swamp in Coral Harbor.

Segments of DANISH PAVING are still intact on some of the old plantation roads.

REMINDERS OF THE PAST

The most obvious reminders of St. John's agricultural past are the traces of the old Danish road system and the ruins of sugar mills, factories, and plantation houses. Although never simultaneously in full operation, over eighty separate cotton and sugar estates have existed on the island, linked by a road system surpassing in extent that of today. This network provided social communication among plantations; but, more importantly, it provided access to the sea for the produce of the upland estates. Down from the island's rugged central ridge, oxcarts laboriously hauled out hogsheads of crude sugar and bulky raw cotton to be loaded on inter-island sloops for transport to Danish West India Company warehouses in St. Thomas.

These roads were simple but skillfully engineered cartways. Unmortared stone retaining walls can still be traced for miles, and in a few prosperous sections the routes were even paved with rough cobblestones. Parts of the main track along the island's crest have evolved into the present Centerline Road; other old tracks are maintained as park trails.

The mills and factory buildings, especially those reconstructed in the later revival of sugar production, were built massively and skillfully, with the very minimum of engineering aids. The ruins at Annaberg, Cinnamon Bay, and Reef Bay all represent extensive reconstruction in the late 1800's upon earlier foundations. The original yellowish hand-made brick and shaped coral were combined with imported Danish red brick and an assortment of other materials, including ballast stones brought in by freight boats from other islands. Brain coral heads, brought fresh from the sea, were relatively easily cut. Hardening as they aged, these beautiful blocks were used in creating the sturdy archways and precise cornerstones of windmill and factory buildings.

Wall built of brain coral and Danish brick

The weakest link in the construction process was the quality of the mortar, often prepared from crushed, burned coral, crude molasses, and brackish water. To protect mortared joints from rapidly eroding away, many of these massive and beautifully composed walls were subsequently plastered over. This was done especially inside the factory buildings themselves to combat the tremendous heat and steamy air over the boiling vats of sugar. Traces of this covering, traditionally painted a pale, rusty red, can still be seen on the Reef Bay factory walls.

Lintels and door frames were fashioned of native woods such as lignum vitae and bulletwood, because of their great strength and resistance to termite attack. A few of these pieces, now nearly a hundred years old, are still in place. Softer woods were generally used for the long structural members such as floor joists in the two-story factories. Most of these are gone now, but the rows of neatly formed support holes now gaping from the massive walls attest to the tremendous strength designed into these floors.

Sometimes the best clue to the location of a former dwelling or factory is the presence of a living memento — an ancient, massive tamarind tree which once shaded a courtyard or kitchen, a lonely royal palm tree once tended by a planter's wife, or a mass of thorny-bladed ground pinquins (a relative of the pineapple) descended from plants once intended as a living fence against intruders.

Ground pinquin

The subtropical vegetation of the Virgin Islands is not kind to the abandoned works of man. In the absence of the almost daily effort needed to fend off the encroaching forest, each available crevice in walls and foundations soon sprouts a seedling tree; vines cover the rest. Termites make short work of all but the most resistant wooden materials. The growing tree roots soon split apart even the most substantial walls, eventually reducing whole buildings to vague jumbled outlines on the shady forest floor.

Termite nest

A NATIONAL PARK

The potential for park development in the U.S. Virgin Islands, including St. John, was recognized by early territorial officials soon after the United States purchased the islands from Denmark in 1917—but the first formal National Park Service appraisal of St. John did not come until 1936. This study, while recognizing the great recreational potential of beach areas and the historical significance of the many plantation ruins, concluded essentially that the altered nature of the biota following sugar agriculture would not qualify the island for national park status.

This assessment was apparently strengthened by a conviction that there would be little commercial development pressure on St. John, and that the beautiful hillsides and watersheds above the island's beaches would remain substantially untouched for many years. In 1936, when only 700 people inhabited St. John, and when no vehicles, paved roads, or powerlines traversed its peaceful slopes, this conviction may have seemed justified.

But in 1939 a second and much more positive National Park Service assesssment was issued. At that junction it was suggested that the whole island be incorporated into a proposed park, with acceptable provisions for the island's people to continue their traditional life styles and at the

same time participate in the commercial services inherent in the development of park facilities.

The park proposal (and St. John itself) received little national interest during the 1940's, while at the same time considerable war-related construction and economic changes were taking place in neighboring St. Thomas.

The early 1950's, however, brought recognition to the tremendously accelerated pace of tourist and commercial development in St. Thomas and the Caribbean as a whole, and the park proposal was re-examined. Private conservation concerns, in particular Laurance Rockefeller and his associates in the Jackson Hole Preserve Corporation, indicated a willingness to donate funds and/or acquire certain property on St. John for the purpose of establishing a national park.

Concurrent with land acquisition by these private parties, legislation was introduced in Congress in 1956 to authorize such a park on the island of St. John. Signed into law by President Eisenhower on August 2, 1956, this legislation authorized the federal government to accept the donation of up to 9,500 land acres on St. John, and also provided that the area be administered by the National Park Service. Congress did not include the whole island in the intended park; the principal population centers of Cruz Bay, Coral Bay, and East End — totaling some 3,000 acres — were excluded.

Jamaican red-tailed hawk

Buildings of an earlier time left unattended soon fall prey to the encroaching forest.

Strangler fig

Formal dedication ceremonies, during which over 5,000 privately purchased acres were transferred to the federal government, took place at the bandstand in Cruz Bay on December 1, 1956. A park in St. John was finally assured!

Within the space of a few years the impact of spearfishing, aquarium-fish collection and other exploitative pressures occurring off the reefs and beaches of the new park were felt, and the omission of these offshore waters from the specific jurisdiction of the Park Service was recognized as a critical oversight. As a result, in 1962 some 5,560 acres of submerged lands off the northern and southern coasts of the island, already under the jurisdiction of the Department of the Interior (owing to the island's status as a U.S. territory), were formally transferred to the supervision of the National Park Service.

Following the original donation of privately purchased lands, further land acquisition by the federal government has progressed slowly. The inevitable spiraling of the value of remaining private lands ("inholdings") within the authorized park area has meant that public funds set aside by Congress in 1962 to complete land acquisition were inadequate. Although new commitments are being sought, land ownership within the park still reflects this serious dilemma. Large inholdings, including five of the principal bays and watersheds of the north shore, still effectively divide the park into separate units.

It seems certain that virtually all remaining private lands on St. John will face development pressures from an external world of increasing affluence, as well as from a growing and aspiring population within. As a responsive and responsible element of Virgin Islands society as a whole, and as a unit of the National Park Service, Virgin Islands National Park faces both a challenge and an obligation: to help ensure that the beauty, charm and uniqueness of St. John—which have themselves created the gathering development momentum — are not lost in the process.

The land, the sea, and a rich cultural heritage are the instruments which have shaped the St. John of yesterday and today. In welcoming a national park, the people of the Virgin Islands have become a vital instrument in the shape of the future.

SUGGESTED READING

BOND, JAMES. *Birds of the West Indies.* London: Collins Company, 1971.

HECKERT, ELEANOR L. *Muscavado.* Garden City, N.Y.: Doubleday & Co., 1968.

JADAN, DORIS. *A Guide to the Natural History of St. John.* St. Thomas: Virgin Islands Conservation Society, 1971.

LEWISOHN, FLORENCE. *Divers Information on the Romantic History of St. Croix.* St. Croix Landmark Society.

WESTERGAARD, WALDEMAR C. *The Danish West Indies under Company Rule.* New York: Macmillan Co., 1917.

Last light of plantation's

Other books in this series: Grand Canyon, Zion, Yosemite, Canyon de Chelly, Theodore Roosevelt, Capitol Reef, Dinosaur, Death Valley, Petrified Forest.

PRINTED BY W. A. KRUEGER CO. PHC